PLAY BY PLAY

TRACK

DISCARD

Thanks to coaches Pat Burns and Kyle Infozato and the following Richfield High School athletes who were photographed for this book:

Pat Akappate
Megan Bielefeld
Bunbob Chun
Pat Doty
Jeff Dowell
Nate Fias
Rachel Gieseke
Joann Htut
Kyle Infozato
Walter James
Nikki Jensen
Ben Johnson
Mike Johnson
Ona Johnson
Kali Kimbrall
Ashley Kleist
Robin Lass
Parker Maretz
Erin Petrik
Megan Petrik
Josefin Petterson
Svetlana Sinykin
Meredith Strom
Brie Waltman

THE EXPANSION OF WOMEN'S TRACK

Women were not even allowed to watch the ancient Olympics. A woman named Hippodameia organized the Hera Games for women spectators and runners. No men were allowed at that event. This separation continued until a young man named Pisidorus entered the Olympics. His mother had finished training him for the games after the death of his father. She dressed as a man in order to watch her son's Olympic race. As she celebrated her son's victory, she came out of disguise. Because the mother had helped her son achieve Olympic glory, officials made an exception for her. Eventually, women were allowed to watch and even take part in Olympic events.

But when the Olympics began again in 1896, women were once again not allowed to compete. In 1928 two track events opened to female athletes: the 100-meter dash (above) and the 800-meter run. Some of the women during the 800-meter run fell to the ground exhausted by the effort. Critics howled that this display of frailty showed that women didn't belong on the track. These same people ignored that men frequently collapsed after a challenging race. Popular opinion was against female athletes. It took many years for women to be accepted in the world of track. But accomplished athletes, such as Betty Robinson (number 879 above), Wilma Rudolph, Babe Didrikson Zaharias, Florence Griffith Joyner, Gail Devers, Jackie Joyner–Kersee, and Marion Jones, have helped pave an enduring track tradition for women runners.

featured 100-meter, 400-meter, 800-meter, and 1,500-meter races, as well as the 110-meter hurdles. In later years, other distances and relays were incorporated. The level of competition at the Olympics has inspired runners to set new standards for running performance. Many athletes begin training at an early age. At every level, athletes don't just race against other people, they race against themselves to achieve their **personal bests.**

Spectators filled the Panathenian Stadium in Athens, Greece, to watch the 1896 Olympic Games. Much narrower than modern tracks, this track had tight curves that were sometimes hazardous to the athletes.

The temple of Hera housed the Olympic wreaths and was the center of women's competitions. The ruins still stand about 110 yards from the location of the ancient Olympic stadium.

Theodosius I, abolished the Olympic Games in A.D. 394 because they honored Greek gods. Footraces continued on a local level.

In particular, the sport met much enthusiasm in Britain. Footraces became popular local events. Throughout medieval times, people gathered to cheer on their favorites at village greens (parks). British colonists brought these contests to the New World. They discovered that native residents already had their own long racing traditions.

By the nineteenth century, races had become a regional spectator sport. Industrialized towns in the United States and Britain formed sports clubs and held races. Some British military schools decided that training for races would help build the character of their future officers. Other prep schools and universities held competitions, called **meets,** in which athletes raced one another. The universities of Oxford and Cambridge held their first competition in 1864. Ten years later, the first American intercollegiate meet was held at Saratoga Springs, New York.

In the late nineteenth century, the excavation of ancient Olympia captured people's imagination and brought about the revival of the Olympics in 1896. Among other events, the first modern Olympiad

events even though people in other parts of the world also raced.

The Olympics began in 776 B.C. as a one-day religious festival for Greek men. Honoring Zeus and other Greek deities, the festival was held in Olympia, Greece, and featured a foot-race. Longer races and other events were eventually added to these Olympic festivals. For most events, the athletes participated barefoot and without clothes—the loincloths usually worn were proven to slow runners down considerably after one man accidentally lost his during a race and won. In one race, however, naked warriors strapped on full armor, including shields, and sprinted down the oval used for chariot races.

By 632 B.C., the games had become a five-day event filled with speeches, feasting, and poetry readings. On the final day, the winners paraded to the temple of Zeus, where they were crowned with wreaths made from olive tree branches. Second- and third-place finishers received no recognition. When the winner returned home, his village or town often showered him with possessions. He was so well taken care of that he didn't need to do anything else for the rest of his life.

The Olympics thrived for over 700 years. When the Romans made Greece part of their empire in 146 B.C., people from other lands around the Mediterranean Sea traveled to Greece to race one another. Eventually, a Christian Roman emperor,

In this drawing of an ancient Olympic footrace, musicians and cheering spectators encourage the shield-carrying runners.

Chapter 1

A HISTORY OF TRACK

People started racing each other to answer one question: Who's the fastest? The sport of track brings different groups of people together to answer that very question. Titles range from the fastest kid in school to the fastest man or woman in the world. The site of the race can range from a gravel playground to a stadium filled with cheering people.

Racing has been around for a long time. Ancient people ran to escape predators or to hunt prey. Speed and agility were greatly admired, not to mention necessary for survival. Staged competitions helped determine who had the most skill in areas related to hunting: running, jumping, and throwing weapons, such as rocks or spears.

Eventually, running events were held only for amusement or for competition's sake. Written records of racing, such as the Tailteann Games in Ireland, date back to the nineteenth century B.C. But most people think of the Olympic Games in ancient Greece as the direct ancestor of modern track

Joining a track team isn't just about competition and being the fastest. Running is good exercise and a great group activity.

7

CONTENTS

For Grandma Edna

This book is available in two editions:
Library binding by LernerSports
Soft cover by LernerSports • FAE
Imprints of Lerner Publishing Group
241 First Avenue North
Minneapolis, MN 55401 U.S.A.

Website address: www.lernerbooks.com

Library of Congress Cataloging-in-Publication Data

Nitz, Kristin Wolden.
   Play-by-play track / by Kristin Wolden Nitz ; photographs by Andy King.
      p.   cm. — (Play-by-play)
   Includes bibliographical references and index.
   ISBN: 0–8225–3936–5 (lib. bdg. : alk. paper)
   ISBN: 0–8225–9873–6 (pbk. : alk. paper)
   1. Track and field—Juvenile literature. I. King, Andy, ill.
II. Title. III. Series.
GV1060.55 .N59 2004
796.42—dc21   2002154875

Manufactured in the United States of America
1 2 3 4 5 6 – JR – 09 08 07 06 05 04

Photo Acknowledgments
Photographs are reproduced with the permission of: © Bettmann/CORBIS, pp. 8, 36, 58; © Hulton Archive by Getty Images, pp. 9, 10, 11; © Mike King/CORBIS, p. 25; © Wally McNamee/CORBIS, p. 41; © CORBIS, p. 46. All illustrations by Bill Hauser.

PLAY BY PLAY

TRACK

Kristin Wolden Nitz
Photographs by Andy King

LernerSports ● Minneapolis

Chapter 2

BASICS

Many middle schools and most high schools and colleges have track teams. In most areas, the track season is in the spring. Members of a track team train together and attend meets together. The running events of a track meet feature races from 100 meters (109 yards) to 3,200 meters (2 miles). Track athletes participate in relay races and hurdles as well.

Track events are divided into categories by length. There are **sprints, middle-distance races,** and **long-distance races.** For younger runners, sprints include the 100-meter dash and the 200-meter dash. Middle-distance races encompass the 400-meter dash and the 800-meter run. The 1,600- and 3,200-meter runs fall under long-distance running. The boundaries of these categories change as athletes advance in age and endurance. (In college, long-distance races start at 5,000 meters!)

Athletes interested in track don't need a lot of special equipment. They only need proper footwear, comfortable clothes, and a place to train.

ATTITUDE

When joining a track team, attitude is everything. Before runners step up to the starting line, they undergo hours of training to improve their endurance, speed, and technique. Some athletes may be tempted to quit after a few sore muscles. Determined runners work hard in practice and learn how to run their races.

SHOES

It's important to start with the right shoes. By design, running shoes cushion the foot in all the right places. Expect track shoes for practicing to be light, but not so light that they don't provide enough support, especially along the arch of the foot. Middle- and long-distance runners need extra support in the heel. They should look for a shoe with a wider sole to help their heels withstand the pounding on the pavement.

When you try on shoes, make sure the heel fits firmly so that it doesn't slip off your foot. Leave a little extra room at the toes, because your feet will swell during a tough workout. Shoes fit everyone differently. Select a shoe based on the size and shape of your foot, not according to what's in style. Some manufacturers' sizes run narrow, and others run wide. If you have a high arch, your foot may require more cushioning.

Many athletes buy a pair of racing shoes for meets. Racing shoes are lighter in weight than training shoes. Sprinters and hurdlers race in shoes that resemble a slipper with spikes under the toes. (Traction at the toes helps runners achieve a quick **take-off.**) A 100-meter sprint shoe has very little cushioning, since the race lasts less than thirteen seconds. Athletes in middle-distance races should choose a shoe that has a full sole but minimal cushioning in the midsole. Long-distance runners need shoes that grip the track and cushion the feet.

Wear your sweat suit during warm-ups and keep it on until a few minutes before your event to guarantee loose muscles.

CLOTHES

Your clothing should be lightweight and wind resistant so that you can cut through the air smoothly. Be careful that your clothing doesn't restrict your freedom of movement. The fabric should also be able to breathe so that sweat can evaporate instead of being trapped against your body. High schools will usually provide uniforms for track meets.

Sweatpants and a sweatshirt are also necessary articles of clothing. They'll keep you warm as you train during the early weeks of the track season. Staying warm also helps your muscles stay loose at a meet as you wait between events.

STARTING BLOCKS

Most competitions require the use of **starting blocks** for races up to and including the 400-meter race. Runners push off from starting blocks with their feet. Runners call this "exploding out of the blocks." There are several kinds of starting blocks. The traditional style has a metal bar with two movable plates, one on each side of the bar. Newer versions have only one movable plate, while the second is attached at the front of the bar. Both of these styles serve the same

Notches in the bar allow the runners to adjust the spacing and position of the plates to suit their preference.

purpose—the plates "block" the runners feet from sliding back on a quick start.

At first, it may feel awkward to get down into the blocks. You may think that your time from a standing start would be much faster, but it's usually not. The starting blocks put runners into an angled, more aerodynamic position, which allows time to build speed before becoming upright. As your technique improves, you will soon learn just how explosive a start from the blocks can be.

THE TRACK

Outdoor tracks are 400 meters (440 yards) around and laid out in the shape of an oval. The oval has two **straightaways** and two curves, which each measure 100 meters. Sprinters in the 100-meter dash run down one straightaway. Athletes in the 3,200 meter race around the track eight times.

Most tracks are outdoors, but there are also indoor tracks. Their circumference is usually 200 meters—3,200 meters is sixteen times around an

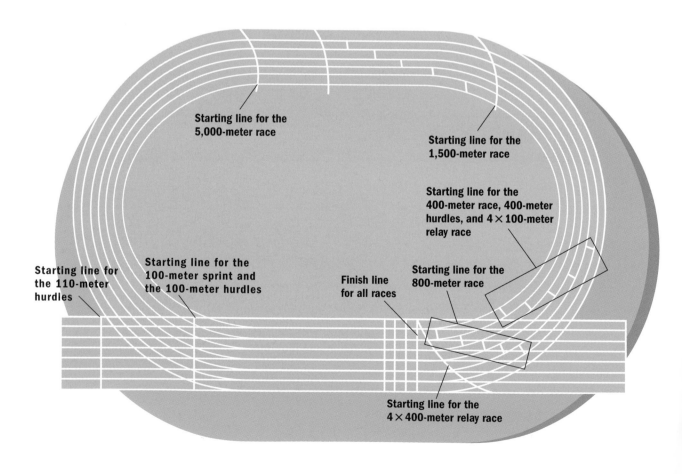

Starting line for the 5,000-meter race

Starting line for the 1,500-meter race

Starting line for the 400-meter race, 400-meter hurdles, and 4 × 100-meter relay race

Starting line for the 110-meter hurdles

Starting line for the 100-meter sprint and the 100-meter hurdles

Finish line for all races

Starting line for the 800-meter race

Starting line for the 4 × 400-meter relay race

indoor track. This book focuses on races run on outdoor tracks.

Both indoor and outdoor tracks have special surfaces. Up until the nineteenth century, races were held on grass tracks. Dirt and cinder tracks, which are mixtures of clay, gravel, and sand, were also popular surfaces and are still used in some places. These days, most tracks are made of synthetic, or human-made, materials. The rubberized surface of a synthetic track lies on top of asphalt and acts as a shock absorber. Synthetic tracks require less upkeep than tracks made of natural materials, whose lines need to be remarked. All track surfaces have markings that indicate starting points for different events: the finish line, zones for passing the baton in relays, and lanes in which to run.

Outdoor tracks have eight lanes. Each lane is 2½ feet wide. Runners receive a lane number. Lane assignments are usually based on the time from your last race. The runners with

the fastest times get **lane priority** and receive the center lanes, which have a better view of the field. The runners with the slowest times will be placed in lanes one and eight.

Runners must stay in their lanes for races that last up to one **lap** around the track. Crossing into another lane is grounds for disqualification. For races longer than 400 meters, runners may leave their lane after the first lap. In those races, the athletes normally steer to the inside of the track. Because the track is an oval, the outside lane is slightly longer than 400 meters.

In races that include a bend in the track, runners start in staggered positions. For instance, the 200-meter race starts on the curve and finishes at the end of the first straightaway. Runners in the outside lanes start farther up than runners in the inside lanes. The lines for a **staggered start** are carefully measured so that all runners, no matter their lane, will race an equal distance.

Chapter 3

WARM-UPS

Each practice begins with warming up, which often consists of jogging, stretching, and drills. Some runners rush through the **warm-ups** and don't realize their importance. Warming up not only prevents injuries, it also cuts down on soreness from intense workouts.

During practices, athletes usually warm up as a team. At a meet, each athlete warms up and stretches in time for his or her race. Ideally, you should finish your series of stretches about fifteen minutes before the start of your event.

Runners should start warm-ups with a slow jog to get blood flowing to the muscles. Only stretch your muscles when they're warm. Moving your arms will get your heart pumping faster. Swing your arms from side to side while rotating your upper body. Then do some upper body exercises. Neck stretches, arm circling, and side bends loosen the muscles in the neck, shoulders, chest, abdomen, and lower back. Runners give extra attention to stretching the muscles in the legs.

Remember three things when stretching: never stretch to the point of pain, breath normally as you stretch, and stretch both sides of the body equally.

STRETCHING

There are many different ways to stretch your muscles. Depending on your personal flexibility, you may need more or less intensive stretches. But whatever stretch you choose, be careful and respect your body and its limitations.

One of the most common running injuries is a pulled or torn hamstring. The hamstring muscle is located at the back of the leg. Erin demonstrates one way to stretch the hamstring muscle (top right). She sits on the ground with both legs extended. She slowly leans forward over her legs and stretches as far as it's comfortable. By flexing her feet—rather than pointing her toes—Erin extends the stretch through her calf muscles.

A variation of the hamstring stretch works one leg at a time. To do this stretch, you extend one leg forward. Pull the foot of your other leg in, so that the sole of your foot touches the inner thigh of your extended leg. As you gradually lean forward, you will feel your hamstring muscle lengthening.

To stretch the quadriceps, the front thigh muscle, Rachel places one hand against a wall for balance (bottom right). She uses the other hand to lift up her foot until it presses against the back of her thigh. She tucks in her pelvis to prevent her back from arching and to increase the stretch. She is

Hamstring Stretch

Quad Stretch

careful not to overextend the knee or strain the quads. This stretch may also be done on the ground instead, as shown by Megan (below).

Walls are also useful for the calf stretch. Nikki stands an arm's length away from the wall (right). She steps back with one foot, bends the front knee, and pushes against the wall. The calves should be stretched at the beginning of practice. Many athletes also look for a wall during and after a hard workout.

Calf Stretch

If you're a hurdler, you may also want to try the hurdler's stretch to stretch the front of your legs. Be extra careful not to overdo this stretch or to twist your knee the wrong way.

DRILLS

Some of the sprinting drills can make the team look like a bunch of escapees from a spring musical. It can be amusing to watch serious athletes skipping down the track, but each drill has its purpose.

The skipping drill (bottom left) uses the same basic skipping motion that everyone learned in preschool. With each skip, you should drive your knees high into the air and swing your arms vigorously.

The high knees drill (bottom right) helps lengthen your **stride,** the distance between the front and back leg. You can try it standing in place or while jogging. One at a time, lift your knees to the level of your hips. Land on the balls of your feet without rocking back to the heel. Drive your arms so that your body stays balanced.

Heel flicks, also known as bottom kicking, will strengthen the hamstring muscle. Moving forward at a slow jog, swing your heel back until your calf presses against your thigh.

Skipping

High Knees

The Grapevine

For the grapevine (above), you will be moving sideways. Begin with your feet together. Pick up your right foot and move it to the right. Next, cross your left foot behind your right one. Push off your left foot and land on your right one. Next, cross your left foot in front of your right foot. Practice this series slowly for a few times before increasing your speed.

Although you will be racing on the track, you won't spend all your training time there. Your coach may send you on a run in the neighborhood, through a local park, or up and down the highest hill in the area. On rainy days, you may even be told to run in the halls of your school.

Chapter 4

SPRINTS

The sprints range from 50 meters (usually only run on indoor tracks) to 100 or 200 meters. Most sprinters prefer one race to another. Mastering two is much more difficult. Very few sprinters have managed to capture the elusive double (competing in the 100-meter and the 200-meter events) at the Olympics. The runners who have achieved this goal include Jesse Owens, Betty Cuthbert, Wilma Rudolph, Carl Lewis, and Marion Jones.

Sprinting demands maximum effort over the entire distance. When the gun goes off, sprinters accelerate to top speed or near top speed and stay there for the duration of the race. The sprint has three phases: the start, the acceleration, and the finish.

MICHAEL JOHNSON

The scheduling of the 200- and the 400-meter events used to conflict. Runners were unable to participate in both races at a single meet. In the 1996 Olympics, Michael Johnson successfully petitioned to have the event times adjusted so that he could compete in both. The officials made the change, and Johnson won two gold medals.

THE START

In the sprints, a good start is critical. Sprinters use starting blocks to push themselves into the race. During race preparations, sprinters arrange the starting blocks. Most sprinters put the front block about two shoe lengths back from the line. The back block goes one shoe length behind the front one.

When Bunbob hears the command "on your marks," he backs into the blocks so that his back knee is even with his front foot. He rests his back knee on the ground and lines up his fingertips behind the starting line.

When told to "get set," Bunbob raises his hips above his shoulders. Most of his weight is now on his fingers. His arms bend slightly at the elbows. Bunbob takes a deep breath and will hold it until the starter fires the gun. He keeps his head low and relaxed. He focuses his eyes in the center of his lane about 3 feet ahead.

The starter fires the gun. Bunbob pushes off with his front foot while driving his back leg forward. He swings the arm on the side of his front foot forward while the opposite arm swings back.

Bunbob's Start

THE ACCELERATION

Bunbob continues to lean forward after he explodes out of the blocks. His knees are high. He drives his arms forward and backward—not across his chest. Bunbob's stride gradually increases as his body straightens. He will be completely up about 20 meters after the start. He continues to run on his toes and the balls of his feet as he accelerates. When he reaches top speed, he switches from accelerating to striding.

THE FINISH

Megan demonstrates the finish (right). Her knees stay high to achieve a long, natural stride. Overstretching the stride results in pushing off the heel, spending more time in the air, and ultimately losing time. On the last stride, Megan pulls both arms back so that her head and shoulders **dip,** or lean, forward to break the tape. Officials pay no attention whatsoever to an athlete's feet, arms, or head. The chest that breaks the tape first wins.

Beginners may approach the finish slightly differently. Since dips can be difficult to master, beginners should pretend that the finish line is 10 meters farther. They run through the tape and only dip in practice, until they master the move.

Runners enter the bend in the track with their left shoulders lower and leaning into the curve. Then they gradually straighten up as they advance through the bend.

TACTICS FOR SPRINTING

You may be tempted to size up your competition before a race. You'll notice that sprinters can be short or tall. Shorter sprinters frequently have a faster start. Taller runners may start more slowly, but their top speed can be faster than that of a shorter runner. Plan to run your own race without looking for or worrying about the other runners.

The 200-meter dash requires more technique than the shorter sprint. In the 200-meter dash, runners only accelerate to a pace that they can maintain all the way to the finish line. During the middle of the race, sprint-ers coast at that top speed. Sprinters begin to tire during the last 70 meters. They work to lift their knees high and pump their arms harder. The faster the arms pump, the faster the legs will go.

Sprints of 200 meters and longer include a run around the bend in the track. These sprints have staggered starts to equalize the distance. But there are even more ways to shave off distance and time. On the bend, be sure to stay close to the inside of your lane to reduce the distance that you need to run. Lean into the bend by driving your right arm harder than your left. Also angle your left shoulder slightly forward.

TRAINING FOR SPRINTERS

Each practice will open with jogging, stretching, and strengthening exercises with the whole track team. Then all sprinters will spend some time endurance running. The distances will be shorter than those of the long-distance runners but much longer than a sprinter's normal race. Although sprinters rely on speed, they, too, have to build endurance. During the endurance run, a sprinter's goal is either plain jogging or running in short bursts at high speeds during the jog, depending on the practice.

At the beginning of the season, coaches will spend time working with their sprinters on their starts and acceleration to correct any problems. Since the winner of a sprint can be measured in fractions of a second, a good, fast start is critical. Later, groups of sprinters will work together, taking turns being the starter. Sometimes the starter will use a noisemaker, called a **clapper,** to imitate the sound of the gun. Practice responding to the noise. Being too anxious will lead to a **false start,** which means crossing the starting line before the gun goes off. Often sprint starts will occur near the beginning of a practice when the runners are still fresh.

FALSE STARTS

Policies vary. Some meet organizers have gone to the strict "no false start" rule where any false start results in immediate disqualification. Other organizers have decided to "charge the false start to the field," which means that all participants are credited with a false start whether they committed it or not. In such cases, any subsequent false start by any runner will be a disqualification. Other sets of rules allow a maximum of two false starts per runner. Be sure you know which rules are in effect for your meet!

Chapter 5

MIDDLE- AND LONG- DISTANCE RACES

In middle school and high school, the 400-meter and 800-meter runs are middle-distance races and the 1,600-meter and 3,200-meter runs are long-distance races. In these races, runners don't accelerate to their top speed as sprinters do. Instead, these runners learn to pace themselves.

Middle-distance runners maintain energy until the end of a race. Then they must sprint. They need to be able to call up extra energy. Both endurance and sprinting ability—sometimes called speed endurance—are necessary for a middle-distance runner.

Long-distance runners rely more on endurance than on speed. They find a steady pace that works for them and stick to it. But even long-distance runners need a burst of speed as they reach the final stretch.

MIDDLE-DISTANCE RACES

Middle-distance races have staggered starting lines and, like the sprinters, sometimes use starting blocks. When the gun sounds, the runners take off fast, but not at full speed. They soon fall into stride.

A middle-distance runner's stride is almost as long as a sprinting stride, but the knees aren't driven as high. You land on the ball of your foot and rock back to the heel before pushing off the ball of your foot once again. Keep your arms relaxed and bent at the elbows. Your hands should be loose and not clenched into fists.

You may not be running much faster in the last 100 meters, but you do have to work harder to maintain your speed. Pump your arms like a sprinter. Run on the balls of your feet. Pretend that the finish line is 10 meters farther down the track and run through the tape.

STRATEGIES FOR THE 400

There are many strategies for races. Some take into consideration weather conditions and a runner's strengths. Some people go fast on the backstretch (the longest straight area). Others prefer to run fast on curves. Your coach should be able to help you tailor a strategy.

In general, establish position after the first turn. You may want to slow down for the second turn to conserve energy for the final push. Since the 400-meter race is run in staggered lanes, don't worry about what the other runners are doing. Plan your own race.

STRATEGIES FOR THE 800

For the first 200 meters of the 800-meter race, runners stick to their lanes. At the signal of an official's flag, runners can cut to the inside of the track. Your position during a race determines the amount of energy that you must spend. You must make a plan and run the kind of race that suits you the best.

Some runners like getting the lead and keeping it. This strategy works well if you can put a little distance between yourself and the pack. When runners bunch together, the person leading needs enough energy to stay in front of the pack. If you want to be in the lead, be prepared to work to keep it.

Other runners, such as Lana and Ona (below), prefer to hang back until they feel that it's time to make their move. They know that if the pace is too fast, they should back off. It's possible to make up a lot of distance in the final kick to the finish line as the front runners begin to fade.

Your coach can help you decide what kind of strategy suits your running style and ability.

It can be very frustrating to be trapped by the pack when you have the energy to break away.

Sometimes a tight pack of runners forms. Being boxed in is a danger of running in the pack. Rules say that you can't cut in front of other runners unless you are two strides in front of them. Bumping and pushing out of the pack won't help you **break away.** Although contact occurs on the international circuit, it isn't tolerated at middle school and high school meets. If you do find yourself surrounded by others, sometimes the best solution is to slow down. While the runners around you adjust to your new pace, you can slip to the outside.

LONG-DISTANCE RACES

In long-distance runs, there are no staggered lanes. The runners start on a straight line or an arc. Each point on the arc is an equal distance from the bend, so there is no advantage in the distance. Sometimes, as in the 3,200-meter run, the runners will be separated into two groups with one set of runners in the outside lanes for the first lap and one on the inside. Then the groups switch.

To start a race on a straight line, a long-distance runner stands with the left foot directly behind the starting line. The right foot is back about the length of a shoe. Since the left foot is in front, the right arm is forward. The starter only gives two signals: get set

and go. At get set, the runner crouches slightly and puts weight on the front foot. At the gun, the runner drives forward with the back leg.

Some runners like getting into the lead and keeping it. They are careful, however, not to set a pace that they can't sustain. Other runners like coming from behind. They make their move in the last lap. Don't speed up when passed unless it is during the last lap or you decide not to allow a runner to make a breakaway. Speeding up and slowing down is bad for your focus. Toward the end of a race, accelerate slowly and steadily.

LACTIC ACID

During intense activity, muscles create lactate, commonly called lactic acid. Lactic acid buildup was once thought to contribute to muscle soreness. Recent discussion, however, tells us that muscles use lactate as fuel in order to postpone fatigue. The intensity of sprinting generates more lactate than middle- or long-distance running. Middle- and long-distance runners set a pace at which muscles can consume the lactic acid that's produced. The more experience your muscles have running, the more efficient they become at using lactate. So get out there and run!

THE DANGERS OF RUNNING IN THE PACK

Perhaps, the most infamous collision occurred in the 1984 Olympics between Zola Budd and Mary Decker. Decker had impressed the world community with her times in the 1,500-meter, 3,000-meter, and 10,000-meter runs. Zola Budd, a young South African, was a fellow runner and one of Decker's fans. Budd made international headlines when she was granted the British citizenship that would allow her to compete in the Olympics. (Because of apartheid, South Africa had been banned from the games since 1960.) The press hyped the upcoming competition between Decker and her famous fan.

Decker took an early lead, but then Budd, who ran barefoot, moved to the front of the pack. At 1,700 meters, Budd began edging toward the inside of the lane. Decker, who was only a step behind the leader, could have nudged Budd to let her know how close they were. Not wanting to be accused of pushing,

Decker slowed her pace instead. Disaster struck as Budd's foot made contact with Decker's thigh. As Budd tried to keep her balance, she drifted even more to the left. Decker spiked Budd's foot and lost her balance. She fell hard onto the field and strained her gluteal muscle. Unable to get up, Decker watched in frustration as the pack moved away. Budd, bleeding and upset, lost ground and finished the race in seventh place.

Budd was first disqualified, but then quickly reinstated as officials viewed the film of the accident. Both Budd and Decker had made mistakes, but neither one was technically at fault. Budd should not have cut in on Decker so quickly, but that was a mistake any beginner could have made. As the more experienced runner, Decker would have been wise to slow down and then make a move to pass on the outside, since there was plenty of time left in the race.

TRAINING

Middle- and long-distance runners approach training differently from sprinters. Sprinters think in terms of time spent training. Middle- and long-distance runners are concerned with how much distance they've covered.

Recuperation running is often used to warm up and cool down. Many coaches like their athletes to begin and end practice by taking a couple of slow laps around the field.

During wind sprints, you run at top speed for a short distance, walk back to the starting line, and then run again. Most long-distance runners will need to use this intense burst of energy at the end of a race.

In interval training, you never drop down to a walk. Instead, you run at a challenging speed for 200 or 400 meters. Then you run the same distance at a slower speed in order to recover.

In **Fartlek** training, you decide when to speed up or slow down by listening to your body. You will gain a better understanding of what your body can and cannot do. Then as the other runners impact your race plan, you will have good knowledge of your options.

Hill running combines strength and endurance training. During a hill run, it won't take long before your legs ache and you begin to breathe harder. Run up and down the bleachers to duplicate this effect in flat areas.

Recuperation running, or slow jogging, stimulates blood flow to the muscles.

Chapter 6

HURDLES

The **hurdles** is one track event that doesn't trace its roots back to the ancient Greeks. It began during the nineteenth century as a jumping event for humans instead of horses. The first hurdles were solid barriers that had been hammered into the ground. Runners could seriously injure themselves on the immovable crosspiece, or horizontal bar.

Modern hurdles tip forward in the direction of the finish line. Knocking a hurdle down once resulted in disqualification, but not any longer. Of all of the track events, the hurdle takes the most technique. Athletes who run hurdles need a good start and excellent flexibility. It also helps to have a certain fearlessness—it's not uncommon for a hurdler to trip.

Hurdle events range in distance. Female athletes race the 100-meter hurdles, and male athletes race the 110-meter hurdles. Both boys and girls run the 400-event. During each race, runners must jump 10 hurdles to finish. Hurdles are spaced approximately 10 yards apart in the 100- and 110-meter runs and 49 yards in the 400-meter run.

HURDLE HEIGHTS

On the hurdle bars, a system of notches or pins makes it possible to raise and lower the crosspiece. Heights of the hurdles vary around the country depending on the length of the race and the age and gender of the athlete. Shorter races have higher hurdles. Longer races have lower hurdles. Girls' heights are shorter than those of boys to accommodate the average height of each gender. For high school varsity boys, the 110-meter hurdles are set to a height of 39 inches and the 300-meter or 400-meter hurdles are set to 36 inches. In the girls' hurdle races, the heights are 33 inches for the 100-meter hurdles and 30 inches for the 300-meter event. Junior varsity heights and middle school heights are lower.

PRACTICE

When approaching the hurdles for the first time, you must pick a **lead leg.** Right-handed people tend to choose the right leg, while left-handed people frequently pick the left leg. Some athletes can use either leg, which can be helpful. But, in general, hurdlers can easily develop a stride and a pace to put their lead leg in jumping position.

To get used to the hurdles, Meredith walks toward a hurdle and passes it on the same side as her lead leg. When she's even with the hurdle, she plants the lead leg, leans forward, and pulls her bent trailing leg over the hurdle (left). When she feels comfortable, she'll try it at a jog. Then she'll be ready to leap over the hurdle with her lead leg extended. Hurdlers spend time perfecting the major phases: the start, the takeoff, and the landing.

THE STARTS

Once you feel comfortable jumping hurdles, work on your start. Like sprinters and long-distance runners, hurdlers have to think about how fast they leave the starting line. They also have to think about how many steps they should take before the first hurdle. Hurdlers work hard to make each start identical. When practicing starts for the 100-meter or 110-meter hurdles, they usually go over the second hurdle before slowing. Then they return to the starting line. (Hurdlers in the longer distances can stop after the first hurdle.)

Spend plenty of time getting used to the hurdles. Practice on the side until you feel confident. The more comfortable you feel with the height and the motion, the easier it will be to jump over the hurdles.

GAIL DEVERS

In 1992 Gail Devers won the 100-meter dash for an Olympic gold medal and the title of the world's fastest woman. A few days later, she lined up in the finals of the 100-meter hurdles with a chance to win a second gold. She approached the tenth hurdle with a commanding lead. Her speed was so great, however, that she arrived at the hurdle sooner than she had anticipated. Her foot struck the hurdle, and she fell.

Devers didn't pound the ground in frustration. Instead, she scrambled across the line and finished fifth. Then she stood up and smiled at the crowd. Devers commented later that there were worse things than to crawl across an Olympic finish line with one gold medal hanging around your neck. Devers's personal history gave her a sense of perspective. Only two years earlier, an illness almost required the amputation of her feet.

THE TAKEOFF

Mike sprints toward the hurdle. He raises his lead leg high and drives himself off the ground with his trailing leg. The arm opposite his lead leg also drives forward. His other arm swings down and back. His lead leg straightens so that his heel sails over the hurdle. He stays as close to the hurdle as possible while going over cleanly. He knows that every extra inch in the air will cost him time.

THE LANDING

Mike bends his trailing leg as it goes over the hurdle. He is careful to turn his toe out instead of down so he doesn't knock over the hurdle. Mike leans his upper body forward to bring the lead leg down quickly, landing on the ball of his foot.

BETWEEN THE HURDLES

For the 100-meter high hurdles, athletes work on their technique so that they take a certain number of steps between each hurdle. This number varies according to the height and stride of each athlete. Younger hurdlers may have to alternate the lead leg from hurdle to hurdle as they grow.

In the longer distances (the 300- or 400-meter race), the hurdles are placed much farther apart. Most runners will not count their steps between hurdles. Because of this, you should be able to lead with either leg. Keep your strides as smooth, rhythmic, and even as possible. An awkward **stutter step** to get your favorite leg in position can cost precious time. There is an advantage leading with the left leg on the bends of the track. Your body will lean to the left and follow the curve more naturally.

Some hurdlers like to think of the motion as running over the hurdle instead of jumping over it.

Chapter 7

RELAYS

Relay races are the only track events in which you race with a team. Four runners make up a relay team, and each member runs a section, or **leg,** of the race. The team whose fourth runner finishes first wins.

The most common relay races are the 4×100-meter, the 4×200-meter, and the 4×400-meter race. For instance, each runner of the 4×100-meter race runs 100 meters for a total race of 400 meters. **Medley relays** don't divide the distance equally among teammates. One of these is the 100×100×200×400-meter relay. It goes twice around the track. Some high school meets include the 4×800-meter relay, but longer distances occur at levels above high school.

To mark changes in runners, a **baton** is passed. The baton is a lightweight, hollow tube. It's important to get used to the baton. In the sprint relays, faster runners can be beaten by better baton passers. A mishandled or dropped baton will usually be the end of the team's chances.

RELAY BATONS

In the early relay races, the incoming runner merely had to slap the hand of the outgoing runner. The judges often had a difficult time telling whether physical contact was actually made. Modern batons are hollow tubes constructed of metal, wood, or plastic. They weigh about two ounces and are often brightly colored to make the job of judging the **exchange** easier.

THE FIRST WOMEN'S GOLD IN TRACK

Betty Robinson was the first American woman to win a gold medal in track and field. The sixteen-year-old had only been running competitively for two years when she qualified for the 1928 U.S. Olympic squad in the 100-meter dash.

Even though her first gold medal was a spectacular feat, Robinson has said that she cherished her second gold medal much more because she had to work for it. Three years after the 1928 Olympics, Robinson was involved in a plane crash. The man who found her lying in an open field took her to the morgue because he thought she was dead. Robinson was in a coma for seven weeks and had a badly damaged knee. After she regained consciousness, it took her two years to learn how to walk again.

Robinson started running again as a form of physical therapy. Initially, she didn't have any thought of competing. But she soon discovered that she still had her natural speed. Because of her bad knee, she couldn't get down into the starting crouch, but she still managed to come in fourth at the 1936 Olympic trials in the 100-meter dash. Although she didn't make it into the 100-meter final, she did win a spot on the relay team. When the favored German team dropped the baton, the U.S. team beat the rest of the field by eight meters.

PASSING METHODS

There are two methods of passing the baton: the **upsweep** and the **downsweep.** The upsweep is the safer pass. It is frequently used when members of the relay team change from week to week. Runners who train together consistently use the downsweep.

For the downsweep (below), the **outgoing runner** holds her arm back with her fingers and thumb pointing backward and her palm facing up. The **incoming runner** slaps the baton down into the other runner's hand. In a long-distance relay, such as the 42800-meter race, the outgoing runner may switch the baton to the left hand in preparation for the exchange. In the shorter relays, switching hands can cost valuable time. Teams using the downsweep usually alternate receiving hands instead of having each individual runner switch the baton from hand to hand.

For the upsweep, the incoming runner starts with her hand at the bottom of the baton. The outgoing runner waits with her hand back and palm down. She closes her thumb and forefinger around the baton. Her remaining fingers clamp down as the incoming runner releases her grip.

Local and international competitions accept both the upsweep and the downsweep (above). The key is for coaches and their athletes to use and perfect whichever method they decide upon.

PRACTICE

During practice, members of the relay team get together to work on their exchanges. In the beginning, they may just stand in a line and work on the proper technique for either an upsweep or a downsweep exchange. They want to get used to the feel of their teammates slapping the baton into their hands.

Next, they practice matching speeds while running around the track. The incoming runner moves a certain distance down the track in order to reach his or her speed. The runners make the exchange. Each team has its code word for the outgoing runner to extend his or her hand for the baton. The incoming runner may yell "hit," "hand," or "now."

The outgoing runner reaches racing speed before slowing down and turning around to repeat the process. Sometimes the first and third runner will simultaneously practice handing off to the second and fourth runners to get the feel for a real meet.

THE START

There is no need to practice a special start for the long-distance relays. The sprint relays start from the blocks, however, and are more awkward because of the baton. Position your feet, body, and one hand in the same way as a regular start. The three outside fingers of your other hand curl around the baton. Put weight on the thumb and pointer finger only.

THE ZONES

The baton must be passed within the 20-meter **changeover zone.** The incoming runner may step outside the zone once the pass has been made. Ten meters before the start of the changeover zone is the **acceleration zone.** In this zone, the outgoing runner matches speeds with the incoming runner.

Before the race begins, the athletes running the second, third, and fourth legs of the relay will set down a small plastic cone called a **check mark.** To do this, the outgoing runner places his or her heel against the beginning of the acceleration zone and walks heel-to-toe along the inside lane line. At the end of the preplanned distance, which was determined at practice, the athlete will set down a small plastic cone. When the incoming runner reaches the check mark, the outgoing runner knows to start running.

In the longer relays, only the first lap is done in lanes. After that, the lead runner's team member lines up in the first lane. Runners watch their handoffs because if any runner chooses to make a move before the handoff, there can be a lot of bumping and switching.

THE SPRINT RELAY

When selecting runners for the 4×100-meter relay, the coach usually picks the fastest runner with the best start to run the first leg. The second and third runners are good at taking and making a handoff. The better bend runner often takes the third leg. The strongest runner is the **anchor,** the runner who finishes the relay.

The outgoing runner, Nikki, looks over her shoulder at the beginning of the acceleration zone. As the incoming runner, Megan, reaches the check mark, Nikki starts running and doesn't look back. She crosses into the changeover zone. Ideally, the exchange should happen near the end of the changeover zone when both runners are at the same speed. Although the runners speed up and slow down, the baton should move at a constant speed. Nikki hears Megan say "hit," and her arm shoots back.

The incoming runner is responsible for the exchange when the outgoing runner is facing forward. This is called a **blind handoff.** Once the incoming runner successfully hands off the baton, she begins to slow down. She stays in her lane until the other runners have moved past her.

DON'T LOOK BACK

It's the classic mistake. Every runner is tempted at one time or another, but don't do it. Don't look back! Turning your head can cost you a fraction of a second. That fraction can cost you the race or a new personal best. So don't worry about what the runner in lane five is doing. Concentrate on running your race in your way.

Chapter 8

THE MEET

A meet can be planned and run with great precision and still look completely chaotic. There's more action than a twenty-ring circus. Some athletes jog slowly around the track for their warm-ups. Relay teams practice their handoffs. A few people do the grapevine across the wide, green infield. As the hurdlers wait, some jump into the air like frogs. Others do high kicks or stretches to warm up their lead legs. Athletes in the field events—such as the high jumpers, the long jumpers, and the pole-vaulters—line up for their turns.

CROSS-TRAINING

At the conclusion of the race, sprinters often hustle back to one of the jumping events. The long jump, triple jump, and high jump are three field events in which a sprinter may participate. During a meet, track events always take priority over field events. It is the responsibility of the athlete to check in with the field events judges and let them know why, when, and how long you will be gone. To minimize interference, events like the high jump and the pole vault, where athletes must clear heights to continue, are frequently scheduled against the long-distance events like the 4×800-meter relay or the 1,600-meter run. The long jump and triple jump are often done "cafeteria style," which means that you may make your four attempts whenever the long jump pits and triple jump pits are scheduled to be open.

The coaches try to schedule the various sprints, runs, and relays so that athletes will have time to rest between their races. Organizers typically allow their athletes twenty minutes to rest from one event to another. The coaches will let their athletes know at what time the events are scheduled, but it is also important to listen to the loudspeaker, which announces a first, second, and final call.

Once the preceding event is complete or the area is clear, the runners report to their lane assignments and adjust their starting blocks. Sometimes, before the athletes are called to their marks, they are allowed a practice start. Once this is complete, the runners remove their sweat suits. When the official announces, "Runners, take your mark," the athletes back into their starting blocks, arrange their fingers behind the starting line, and let their right or left knees rest on the ground.

Once all the racers have settled themselves into their blocks, the official says "Get set." In what looks like a choreographed motion, runners in lanes one through eight raise their back knees off the ground.

As the gun goes off, the athletes launch themselves forward. A burst of noise from the stands follows as fans cheer on their favorite runner. Sometimes the starter fires a second shot immediately following the first. This signals a false start.

Depending on the rules of the meet, the runner who left the starting blocks early will either be disqualified or be allowed one more chance. Sometimes the first false start is "charged to the field," and everyone receives a mark against them. When that occurs, the second start tends to be much slower. In 800-meter and 1,600-meter races, hardly any false starts happen. In fact, the starter usually only says "Runners, take your marks" before firing the pistol. Sometimes fans or teammates station themselves at various stages along the infield to show their support.

In a long-distance race, a coach might stand along the first turn with a stopwatch and call out advice. Just before the lead runner begins the last lap of the 1,600-meter or the 3,200-

meter race, an official often rings a bell. The people in the stands, who have been pacing themselves too, start cheering loudly again as the long-distance runners call up inner reserves of strength to race to the finish.

The relay team checks in as a group. In the 400-meter relay, all four runners stand in their assigned lane with the anchor in the lead and the starter at the end. At a signal from the officials, as many as thirty runners walk forward. The person who runs the first leg stops at the starting blocks. Additional runners are left behind at each changeover zone. It may seem slightly ridiculous, but athletes running the anchor leg must walk three-fourths of the way around the track to take their positions.

Because this runner is in first place in the relay, he and his teammate will make their exchange in lane one.

It takes time for runners to practice their starts and to arrange their check marks. Judges at the start, finish, and exchange zones raise their flags to indicate that everyone is ready. The starter's pistol fires. The crowd cheers. There's a blur of action during the first exchange. Judges watch carefully to ensure that each handoff is made in the changeover zone. A mishandled baton will lose a relay team precious seconds and strides, but a dropped baton means the end of the race.

For longer relays, like the 1,600-meter relay and the 4×800-meter relay, only the first lap is run in assigned lanes. After the first exchange, runners may cut right to the inside lane provided they do not interfere with any other runner. For all other exchanges in the longer relays, the incoming runners take whichever lane is equivalent to their position in the race. For example, the first-place runner stays in lane one. The other runners, who would also have been hugging the inside lane, must fan out to lanes two through eight. Because the incoming runners are typically at the end of their strength, the outgoing runner will not accelerate to top speed before grabbing the baton.

As much as you'd like to cheer for your teammates as they participate in relays or individual races, it's more important for you to rest, relax, and prepare yourself mentally for your own race. After you are finished for the day, you can watch your friends compete. Or you can pick a race or two that you really want to see. Athletes often bring books, decks of cards, and even pillows to keep them-selves occupied and comfortable during the long periods of waiting. At meets that last all day, some track teams either pitch a tent or find a patch of shade where they can lay out their blankets and beach towels.

Early in the season, as your coach determines the strengths of you and your teammates, you may find yourself running in a different set of races each week. Even though runners compete as individuals, their point totals for finishing in first, second, or third add up for their teams. Coaches will shift their athletes from event to event in order to challenge and assess runners as well as to maximize totals for the team competition.

Some runners find they have the explosive speed required for the 100-meter or 200-meter races. Others may feel ready to collapse at the end of a 400-meter race but can handle the different pace of the 800-meter or 1,600-meter races without any trouble. Different combinations of runners will be tried in the various relays. Hurdlers will gain experience in the high hurdles and the 300-meter event.

As the season progresses, athletes who participate in track can measure their increased speed and endurance by the gradual lowering of their race times. But the lessons learned in the oval about dedication, self-awareness, and how to win and lose graciously can be transferred into real life. They can help you get off to a fast start as you prepare to hurdle the obstacles that are set up in front of you.

EDWIN MOSES

The 400-meter high hurdles is an event that demands speed, endurance, and coordination. Edwin Moses dominated this event for years and put together an amazing 107-race winning streak. The 1976 Olympics in Montreal, Canada, was his first international meet. He was a self-coached athlete from a college in the southern United States that didn't even have a track team. Moses went on to win medals in the 1984 Olympics and to set many world records.

TRACK TALK

acceleration zone: the area in which the outgoing runner in a relay matches the speed of the incoming runner

anchor: the runner in a relay race who runs the last section of the race

baton: a hollow tube carried by and passed between relay runners

blind handoff: a relay runner's reception of the baton without looking over his or her shoulder

break away: a long-distance runner's acceleration away from the pack

changeover zone: the length of track in which the baton may be passed from the incoming runner to the outgoing runner

check mark: the spot or the marker on the track that the incoming runner in a relay will reach before the outgoing runner takes off

clapper: a noisemaking device that takes the place of the starting gun in practice

dip: the action done by a runner, as he or she crosses the finish line, in order to push the chest past the rest of the body

downsweep: a relay handoff in which the relay runner grabs the baton with his or her palm up

exchange: when members of a relay team pass the baton to mark the beginning of a new runner and a new leg of the race

false start: the act of leaving the starting blocks before the starter's gun fires

Fartlek: a Swedish word meaning "speed play," a method of training in which the athletes decide how fast or slow to run based on how they feel

hurdles: a race in which runners must jump over obstacles

incoming runner: the runner who hands the baton to the outgoing runner in a relay race

lane priority: the system of assigning lanes according to an athlete's previous performance at a meet

lap: once around the track

lead leg: the leg that goes over the hurdles first

leg: a section or part of a relay race

long-distance race: a race that is longer than 800 meters

medley relay: a relay race that combines different distances

meet: a competition involving more than one group of track and/or field athletes

middle-distance race: in most divisions of middle school and high school athletics, a 400-meter race and an 800-meter race

outgoing runner: the runner who receives the baton from the incoming runner in a relay race

personal best: an individual's best officially measured performance for height or distance

sprint: an event of 50, 100, or 200 meters

staggered start: starting runners in lanes at different points along a curved track so that each athlete will run the same distance

starting block: a piece of equipment from which a runner pushes off at the start of a race

straightaway: the portion of the track that is not curved

stride: the comfortable distance between a runner's feet as they transfer contact with the ground

stutter step: a runner's momentary break of stride

takeoff: when a runner leaves the starting line and accelerates to full speed

upsweep: a relay handoff in which the relay runner grabs the baton with his or her palm down

warm-up: a series of aerobic exercises, drills, and stretches

FURTHER READING

Aaseng, Nathan. *Track and Field*. San Diego, CA: Lucent Books, 2002.

Blackall, Bernie. *Track and Field*. Chicago: Heineman Library, 1999.

Hughes, Morgan E. *Track and Field*. Vero Beach, FL: Rourke Press, 2001.

Jackson, Colin. *The Young Track and Field Athlete*. New York: Dorling Kindersley Limited, 1996.

Kristy, Davida. *Coubertin's Olympics*. Minneapolis, MN: Lerner Publications Company, 1995.

Manley, Claudia B. *Competitive Track and Field for Girls*. New York: Rosen Central, 2001.

McMane, Fred. *Superstar's of Men's Track and Field*. Philadelphia, PA: Chelsea House, 1998.

Nitz, Kristin Wolden. *Play-By-Play Field Events*. Minneapolis, MN: LernerSports, 2004.

Rutledge, Rachel. *The Best of the Best: Track & Field*. Brookfield, CT: Millbrook Press, 1999.

Thompson, Luke. *Track and Field: Track Events*. New York: Children's Book Press, 2001.

Wickham, Martha. *Superstars of Women's Track and Field*. Philadelphia, PA: Chelsea House, 1997.

WEBSITES

American Track & Field
<http://www.american-trackand-field.com/>

Distance Running
<http://www.usaldr.org/>

International Association of Athletics Federations
<http://www.iaaf.org>

Runner's World
<http://www.runnersworld.com>

Time-to-Run
<http://www.time-to-run.com>

USA Track & Field
<http:// www.usatf.org>

INDEX

ABOUT THE AUTHOR

Kristin Wolden Nitz is a substitute teacher
and children's author. When she ran track,
her favorite distance was the 800-meter run.
She holds a degree in electrical engineering
from Michigan Technological University.
Since graduating from college, she has lived
in Connecticut, Florida, New York, Washington
State, Nebraska, and Italy. She lives in
Missouri with her husband and
three children.